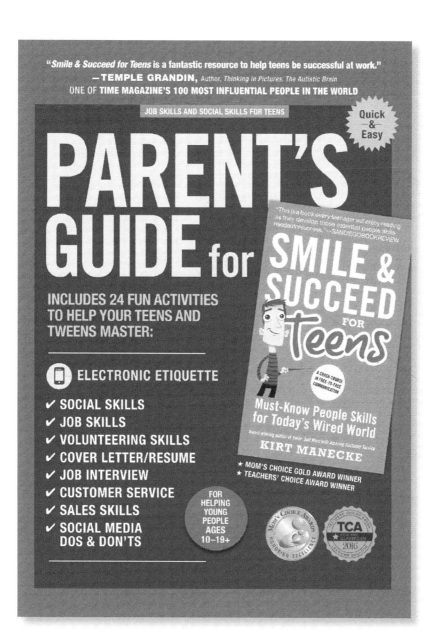

"*Smile & Succeed for Teens* is a fantastic resource to help teens be successful at work."
—TEMPLE GRANDIN, Author, *Thinking in Pictures, The Autistic Brain*
ONE OF **TIME MAGAZINE'S 100 MOST INFLUENTIAL PEOPLE IN THE WORLD**

JOB SKILLS AND SOCIAL SKILLS FOR TEENS

Quick
-&-
Easy

PARENT'S GUIDE for

SMILE & SUCCEED FOR Teens

"This is a book every teenager will enjoy reading as they develop those essential people skills needed for success." —SANDIEGOBOOKREVIEW

A CRASH COURSE IN FACE-TO-FACE COMMUNICATION

Must-Know People Skills for Today's Wired World

Award-winning author of *Smile: Sell More with Amazing Customer Service*

KIRT MANECKE

★ MOM'S CHOICE GOLD AWARD WINNER
★ TEACHERS' CHOICE AWARD WINNER

INCLUDES 24 FUN ACTIVITIES
TO HELP YOUR TEENS AND
TWEENS MASTER:

📱 ELECTRONIC ETIQUETTE

✔ SOCIAL SKILLS
✔ JOB SKILLS
✔ VOLUNTEERING SKILLS
✔ COVER LETTER/RESUME
✔ JOB INTERVIEW
✔ CUSTOMER SERVICE
✔ SALES SKILLS
✔ SOCIAL MEDIA
   DOS & DON'TS

FOR
HELPING
YOUNG
PEOPLE
AGES
10–19+

MOM'S CHOICE AWARD
HONORING EXCELLENCE

TCA
2016

**SOLID
PRESS**
LLC

Also by Kirt Manecke:

Smile & Succeed for Teens:
Must-Know People Skills for Today's Wired World

———

The Teaching Guide for Smile & Succeed for Teens:
Must-Know People Skills for Today's Wired World

———

Smile: Sell More with Amazing Customer Service

———

The Teaching Guide for Smile:
Sell More with Amazing Customer Service

Published by Solid Press, LLC. Inquiries about this book should be addressed to the publisher: Solid Press, LLC, PO Box 145, Milford, MI 48381, kirt@smilethebook.com or 248-685-0483.

www.smilethebook.com

Legal Notice
Please note that much of this publication is based on personal experience that has worked for the author. Your particular situation may not be exactly the same, and you should adjust your use of the information accordingly. Nothing in this book is meant to replace legal/professional advice.

Book Design: Becky Terhune
Book Layout Design: Ariana Abud
Illustrations: Andre Jolicoeur

ISBN:978-0-9850762-8-3

A portion of the proceeds from the sale of this book is donated to animal welfare.

*Dedicated to all the hard-working
parents and grandparents ensuring a brighter
future for teens and young adults.*

C☺NTENTS

INTRODUCTION ....

Chapter 1: Discover Essential People Skills 1

    Learn Essential People Skills.. 2

    Communicate with Adults.. 3

Chapter 2: Make a Powerful First Impression 4

    Master The Top Ten People Skills.................................... 5

    Role-Play Scenarios: The Top Ten People Skills.................. 6

    Role-Play Scenarios A and B 8

Chapter 3: Be Your Own Boss 10

    Create a Flyer 11

    Teen Job Opportunities Worksheet................................. 12

Chapter 4: Land a Job 13

    Create a Cover Letter and Resume................................. 14

    Sample Resume 15

    Fill Out a Job Application.. 16

    Dress for Success 17

    Mock Job Interview 18

    Interviewer Evaluation Worksheet 19

    Bonus Worksheet for Stressful Interview Questions 20

    Sample Prompts to Interview Questions........................... 21

    Keep Your Job.. 23

Chapter 5: Overcome Stress.. 24

    Overcome Stress Evaluation 25

    Overcome Stress Evaluation Worksheet 26

Chapter 6: Master Electronic Etiquette 28

    Use Electronics Responsibly 29

    Professional Electronic Etiquette................................. 30

    Social Media Tips.. 33

Chapter 7: Deliver Amazing Customer Service...................... 34

    Role-Play Customer Service Skills 35

    Customer Service Scenarios 36

    Answer the Phone with a Smile 37

    Answer the Phone with a Smile Sample Dialogues............ 38

    Be a Mystery Shopper Activity 40

    Be a Mystery Shopper Worksheet................................. 41

Chapter 8: Volunteer Effectively 42

    Boost Your Fundraising Skills 43

    Role-Play: Ask for the Donation................................... 44

    Make an Impact: Volunteer 45

Chapter 9: Make it Stick.. 46

    What Have You Learned?.. 47

    Fun Quiz: Test Your Teen's Knowledge.......................... 48

    Review the Book... 50

Book Report 51

Note from the Author.. 52

About the Author... 53

Notes 54

A NOTE FROM KIRT

Thank you for bringing *Smile & Succeed for Teens* into your home. This *Parent's Guide for Smile & Succeed for Teens* will help you be involved in teaching the important social skills and job skills to your tween, teen, and/or young adult. It's quick and easy, just like the book! You will help your teen learn critical skills while boosting their confidence.

Have fun as you help your teen learn skills that will benefit them in school, work, and life. As a parent, you can play a vital role in teaching your teenager these skills and helping with the application. It's a great way to bond with your kids too!

> ***Kirt Manecke***
> Author

HOW TO USE THIS PARENT'S GUIDE

You can choose one or more activity and exercise to do per day, per week, per month, or in whatever order works best for you and your teen.

INTRODUCTION

This *Parent's Guide for Smile & Succeed for Teens* will help you:

- Assist your teen or tween in applying the techniques in *Smile & Succeed for Teens*.

- Engage, practice, and role-play the activities with your son or daughter to help them master communication skills.

- Prepare your teen for a job and give them a head start in their career.

- Help teens who have jobs or who volunteer improve their customer service skills and increase their sales or donations.

AWARD WINNER!

Winner of the prestigious Mom's Choice Gold Award honoring excellence in family friendly products, and the IPPY Gold Award recognizing excellence.

- Winner Teachers' Choice Award
- Winner Mom's Choice Gold Award
- Winner IPPY Gold Award

PRAISE FOR *SMILE & SUCCEED FOR TEENS*

"It is the execution of common people skills which make a difference in the customer experience. *Smile & Succeed for Teens* tackles these issues. You got it right!"

> **ROBERT LAMEIER**
> President & CEO Miami Savings Bank
> Miamitown, OH

"Your book is ALL THE RAGE!"

> **TAMMY HANSFORD**
> Teacher Consultant Washtenaw ISD
> Ann Arbor, MI

"*Smile & Succeed for Teens* is a fantastic resource to help teens be successful at work."

> **TEMPLE GRANDIN**
> Author, Thinking in Pictures,
> The Autistic Brain
> **One of TIME Magazine's**
> **100 Most Influential People in the World**

"What a wonderful read! Easy, practical lessons and tips are sure to catapult your teen into successful work and life relationships! Worth every penny! Buy two & give one to your niece or nephew too!"

> **JOEL KATTE**
> School Principal, Father
> Lexington, KY

Chapter 1

Discover Essential People Skills

LEARN ESSENTIAL PEOPLE SKILLS
From Chapters 1-7 of the book *Smile & Succeed for Teens*

Be certain your teen has their own copy of the book *Smile & Succeed for Teens*.

A smile is powerful!

• Before reviewing the chapters in *Smile & Succeed for Teens*, have your teen brainstorm their ideas and come up with a list of people skills.

• Go over the chapters together, then discuss the merits of each skill and compare to your teen's list. Did your teen learn any new skills? Ask your teen, "Which skills are most important and why?"

FUN QUIZ

Ask your teen: "How quickly do first impressions occur?"

A.   20 minutes
B.   Three meetings
C.   Instantly or within two seconds
D.   Five minutes

CORRECT ANSWER: C. Instantly or within two seconds.
Learn more on page 8 in *Smile & Succeed for Teens*.

> **Ask your teen to brainstorm with you the skills they feel are important to communicate effectively. You or your teen may want to write these down using the "NOTES" pages at the end of this book. These could be skills such as good eye contact, a friendly smile, a firm handshake, proper body language, etc.**

COMMUNICATE WITH ADULTS

Your teen will gain awareness of the importance of people skills when communicating with adults.

Ask Your Teen: "Think about a recent time in your life when you felt awkward around adults. Some examples are: a wedding ceremony and/or reception, a funeral, or meeting adult acquaintances of a family member for the first time. Tell me about the event. Describe the actions of the adults and how you reacted." (Parent may share an event from their teen years as an example.)

• Discuss essential people skills and your teen's experience during that event. Here are some suggestions on how to guide your discussion:

   ✓ Describe actions that illustrate good people skills used by the adults and your teen.
   ✓ Describe actions that did not illustrate good people skills used by the adults and your teen.
   ✓ What does a lack of people skills look like to adults? To parents? To other teens?
   ✓ What could have been done to improve communication?
   ✓ Have your teen describe how they could have used good people skills to improve communication at their event.

Good eye contact makes a powerful first impression.

Chapter 2

Make a Powerful First Impression

MASTER THE TOP TEN PEOPLE SKILLS
From Chapter 1 of the book *Smile & Succeed for Teens*

Role-playing is an effective way for teens to become comfortable with the methods in the book, gain confidence, and obtain desired results. Your teen will practice and role-play **THE TOP TEN PEOPLE SKILLS** as presented in *Smile & Succeed for Teens*. Use the **ROLE-PLAY SCENARIOS** on the next four pages.

• After reading each section in Chapter 1 in *Smile & Succeed for Teens*, your teen will partner with you or another teen to practice that skill. Give feedback and assist as needed.

• Discuss with your teen which people skills they felt most and least comfortable practicing and why.

Too Tight!

A firm handshake says: I'm confident, assertive, and professional.

Too Loose...

Just Right!

QUICK TIP: There are many exercises that can be found in the book in the "Here's How" contained at the end of each chapter. Simply reading these back and forth with your teen is another excellent way to help them learn. For example, "Here's How" sample dialogue can be found on pages 8, 10, 17, 20, 22, and 27 in the **TOP TEN PEOPLE SKILLS** in *Smile & Succeed for Teens*.

Role-Play Scenarios: The Top Ten People Skills

1 **Smile:** Say hello to your teen without smiling, or if there are two teens present have them say hello to each other without smiling. Then say hello to your teen while smiling, or have the two teens say hello to each other with a smile. Ask your teen to compare and contrast their response and reaction during the two experiences.

2 **Make Good Eye Contact:** Have your teen introduce themselves to another teen or to you while making consistent eye contact. Example, "Hello, my name is_____. I am a _____(sixth)_____ grader at _____(school)_____ and my favorite subject is___(science)___ because___(I love nature)_____."

3 **Turn Off the Electronics:** Have your teen take out their cell phone or other favorite electronic device and turn them off for the rest of the day. Next, challenge your teen to turn off their phone the next time they are together with friends, or when your family sits down for a meal!

4 **Say Please and Thank You:** Your teen will ask you or another teen for an item. You or another teen will hand the item to them. Make sure that they are saying "please," "thank you," and "you're welcome" (NOT "no problem" or "yep") during these exchanges. Ask your teen to use these words anytime they make or grant a request.

5 **Shake Hands Firmly:** Model with your teen what "too tight," "too loose," and "just right" looks like. Have them practice with you using the sentence: "Hello, my name is___(your teen's name)___. It's nice to meet you_____(your name)_____." Have your teen shake your hand as a final test (while making good eye contact!).

6 **Introduce Yourself: Make a Friend:** Have your teen pair up with you or another teen. Practice shaking hands, introducing themselves, and asking questions such as: "How's your day going?," "Where have you been on vacation?," "What is your favorite subject?," "What extracurricular activities are you involved in?"

7 **Pay Attention:** Have your teen talk about their favorite place to go on vacation, type of music, band, book, sport, or hobby. Listen without saying anything. After your teen finishes speaking, summarize the main points to show how you were paying attention. Then reverse the roles.

8 **Be Enthusiastic:** Read a short news article or paragraph to your teen in a monotone voice. Ask your teen to describe their reaction. Read it again with an enthusiastic voice. Ask your teen to describe the difference. Have your teen practice speaking with enthusiasm from the author's personal narratives (located in shaded gray boxes) in *Smile & Succeed for Teens*.

9 **Ask Questions:** Have your teen write six questions. Have them analyze each question: Which questions could be answered in a single word? Which questions would inspire further discussion? Have your teen rewrite any close-ended questions as open-ended questions following the examples on page 26 in *Smile & Succeed for Teens*.

10 **Practice Proper Body Language:** Ask your teen to demonstrate improper body language and talk about what message these signals are sending to other people. Then have them demonstrate proper body language following the "Here's How" found on page 27 in *Smile & Succeed for Teens*.

SCENARIO A

DISCUSS AND ROLE-PLAY:

Ted is sitting at a table and face-to-face with his family at a restaurant.

Inappropriate Communication:

While Ted is talking to his mom, he pulls his cell phone out of his pocket, looks down, and quickly checks for messages. Then he puts his cell phone back in his pocket. He does this every 5 minutes.

Professional Communication:

Ted is talking to his mom uninterrupted while making consistent eye contact. His phone is turned off and either left at home or put away.

QUIZ:

You are at the dinner table at home with your family and your cell phone rings, pings, or vibrates. What do you do?

Correct Answer: Ignore it.

ROLE-PLAY:

Assign another teen or yourself as a partner. Role-play having a conversation with a friend, an adult, or a customer. During the conversation their cell phone rings, pings, or vibrates. The teen should ignore their cell phone, maintain eye contact, and continue the conversation.

Role-Play Scenarios

SCENARIO B

Amber is at work and it is slow.

Amber is behind the counter at a retail store where she works. There are no customers in the business. She is tempted to pull out her cell phone and start texting, checking emails, and searching the Internet.

Ask Your Teen: "What should she do?"

Correct Answer: Her cell phone should either be left at home or turned off. She should NEVER check her cell phone at work whether customers are present or not.

Ask Your Teen: "Why not?"

Correct Answer: Using your cell phone at work is a bad habit. It creates a terrible first impression for the customers.

Ask Your Teen: "If you were in Amber's situation, what could you do instead?"

Correct Answer: Do some cleaning, ask your supervisor what you can do to help when the business is slow, learn about the products or services you are selling (read brochures, product boxes, product literature, hang tags, etc.), read and study the menu, call customers who need to be contacted, etc. Having a plan for down time at work will help you become a better, more productive employee and help you form good habits that will benefit you for life.

QUICK TIP: In case of an emergency, make sure you know the name, address, and phone number of the business where your teen is working.

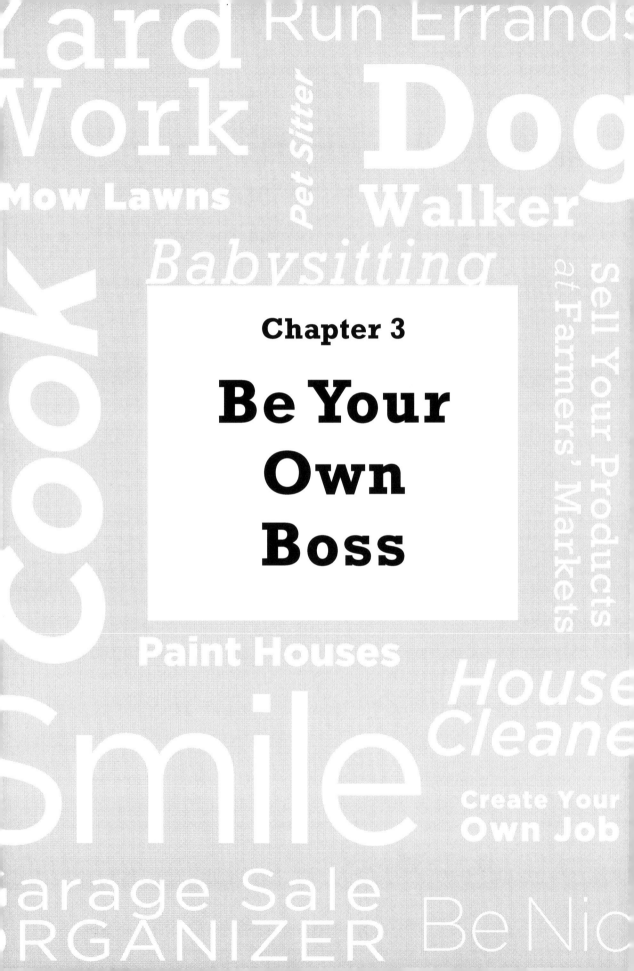

Chapter 3

Be Your Own Boss

CREATE A FLYER
From Chapter 2 of the book *Smile & Succeed for Teens*

Your son or daughter will explore their marketable skills and create a flyer for their own business or service that showcases those skills.

- Ask them to brainstorm a list of businesses or services needed in the marketplace. Discuss the skills/training/education and time necessary for these.

- Using information from the brainstorm session, have them fill in the **TEEN JOB OPPORTUNITIES WORKSHEET** on the next page.

- Show examples of business flyers (visit www.smilethebook.com and click on "FREE"). An example can also be found on page 36 in the book *Smile and Succeed for Teens*.

- Discuss important details about each flyer that will attract customers: pictures/illustrations, headline, features/benefits, bullet points, phone number, and email.

- To create their own job and get the word out to potential customers, your teen will create a flyer based on a job opportunity identified in their **TEEN JOB OPPORTUNITIES WORKSHEET**. They can use a computer or draw by hand.

☺ TEEN JOB OPPORTUNITIES WORKSHEET

My Marketable Skills	Teen Jobs I Can Create or Businesses I Can Start	Additional Skills I May Need

Chapter 4

Land a Job

CREATE A COVER LETTER AND RESUME
From Chapter 2 of the book *Smile & Succeed for Teens*

Your son or daughter will create a cover letter and resume that will help them land a job.

- Share examples of resumes.

- Your son or daughter will type his or her own resume using the **SAMPLE RESUME** on the next page as a guideline.

- Find more examples of resumes at www.smilethebook.com and click on "FREE."

- Find examples of cover letters and the cover letter template at www.smilethebook.com and click on "FREE." There are a multitude of choices on the website, including examples for summer jobs.

A professional-looking
cover letter and resume
will impress employers.

QUICK TIP: Check that the voicemail message on your phone is professional. If a prospective employer calls you, a professional message will ensure that you make a great impression.

 **SAMPLE RESUME**

Amy Smith

123 Main Street • New York, New York 55555

Home: 555-555-5555 • Cell: 555-555-5555 • Email: 123@gmail.com

---

EDUCATION

Westwood High School, Westwood, NY

2015–Present

EXPERIENCE

Dog Walker

2014–Present

- Responsible for exercising customers' dogs and keeping pet supplies full (water, food).
- Experienced in sales. Developed current customer list of five satisfied customers.

Babysitter

2012–2014

- Provided child care for families on evenings and weekends.
- Created educational and fun reading activities for children to help them improve their reading abilities while providing enjoyable entertainment.
- Provided excellent customer service.

ACHIEVEMENTS

DECA: 2017, Academic Honor Roll: 2017, Perfect attendance: 2015, 2016

VOLUNTEER EXPERIENCE

Meals on Wheels, Westwood Animal Shelter, Susan G. Komen Race for the Cure

ACTIVITIES

Girl Scouts, tennis team, school band

TECHNOLOGY SKILLS

Proficient with Microsoft Office, Internet, social media, and WordPress

FILL OUT A JOB APPLICATION
From Chapter 2 of the book *Smile & Succeed for Teens*

Pick up a copy of a job application from a local business or download and print a sample job application on the "FREE" page at www.smilethebook.com.

Have your teen practice filling out a job application.

Here are some tips:

- Write neatly and use proper grammar.

- Fill out the job application completely.

- Check your spelling.

- Don't use acronyms, text abbreviations, or slang.

- Have an adult look over the application for any errors you may have missed.

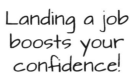

Landing a job boosts your confidence!

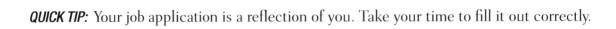

QUICK TIP: Your job application is a reflection of you. Take your time to fill it out correctly.

☺ DRESS FOR SUCCESS

Impress your interviewer.
Be prepared!

MOCK JOB INTERVIEW
From Chapter 2 of the book *Smile & Succeed for Teens*

Your teen will experience the interview process by role-playing as both the interviewer and the interviewee.

- After they read INTERVIEW LIKE A PRO in Chapter 2 of *Smile & Succeed for Teens*, have them practice the interview process with you or another teen using the **INTERVIEWER EVALUATION WORKSHEET** on the next page.

- As the interviewee, have your teen follow the guidelines found in pages 39-40 of *Smile & Succeed for Teens*. Then switch roles and let your teen be the interviewer.

- Evaluate his or her performance.

- Discuss the interview. How could he or she improve?

- Have your teen critique the interview.

- Perform a phone interview asking the same questions. Then switch roles and let your teen be the interviewer. This is an opportunity to discuss the differences between a phone interview and an in-person interview.

- You may want to record the interview by video so you can watch it and make any needed improvements.

Optional: Ask your teen to dress in interview clothes to show him or her what would be acceptable attire to wear during an interview. Practice makes perfect!

QUICK TIP: Explain to your son or daughter that rejection is a part of life and a large part of the job search process. Tell them: "Keep thinking positively and never give up. In the interview, think about how you can help the employer. This will help improve your chances of being considered for the job."

☺ INTERVIEWER EVALUATION WORKSHEET

Interviewer Evaluation

Interviewer: _____   **Interviewee:** _____

(Name)   (Name)

First Impression: ✔ Check all that apply

_____ On time

_____ Dressed for success

(Parent Discretion)

_____ Shirt tucked in

_____ Hair neat and out of face

_____ Fresh breath

_____ Resume with references

_____ Smile

Interviewer Questions:

• Tell me about yourself.

• Why do you want to work here?

• What is your greatest strength/weakness?

• Tell me about your previous work experience.

• How many hours per week can you work?

• When are you available to work? Days? Hours?

• What skills do you have that apply to this job?

• What personal skills do you have that will make you a good employee?

• What questions do you have for me?

Interview Like A Pro: ✔ Check all that apply

_____ Good eye contact

_____ Electronics off/out of sight

_____ Used "please," thank you," and "you're welcome" when appropriate

_____ Firm handshake

_____ Paid attention

_____ Enthusiastic

_____ Sits up straight

_____ No gum

Interviewee Questions:

_____ What are you looking for in an employee?

_____ When can I expect to hear from you?

See sample prompts on page 21.

QUICK TIP: Encourage your teen to job shadow. Explain to them the following: "Spend a half or a full day shadowing someone in a career you are interested in. This way you can see first-hand what the job entails and if it is a job you would like. This insight is invaluable and can save you from investing a lot of time and money in the wrong career."

☺ BONUS WORKSHEET FOR STRESSFUL INTERVIEW QUESTIONS

Sample Interview Questions:

- Why aren't you working right now? Can you explain the gaps in your resume?

- How would you handle a customer complaint?

- Are you available to work weekends and holidays?

- What does your online presence say about you?

- Where do you see yourself in five years?

- Do you get along well with others?

- Tell me about a difficult challenge you had at work and how you completed the task effectively.

- Sometimes, if customers are still present in our business after we close, we have to stay late to assist them. How would you feel about this?

- Are you comfortable selling? If so, please explain.

- What do you think you would like best about working here if you get this job?

- Why should I hire you?

- How would you handle a situation with another co-worker who may disagree with you?

- What do you know about our company?

Interview Like a Pro Checklist

How well did the interviewee conduct themselves during the interview?
Place a ✔ next to each tip that was used.

_____ Be prepared to describe yourself in a few sentences.

_____ Be prepared to explain why you are interested in the job.

_____ Highlight skills and experiences you bring to the job or want to learn.

_____ Answer questions honestly. Don't exaggerate or make things up.

_____ When the interviewer asks if you have any questions, ask about the job and its responsibilities.

_____ Thank the interviewer. Smile, make good eye contact, and shake hands firmly.

☺ SAMPLE PROMPTS TO INTERVIEW QUESTIONS

Some suggestions may or may not apply to your teen. Depending on the type of job your teen is applying for, these could be acceptable answers. Please ask your teen to only use these answers if they are appropriate and apply to them. Remind your teen to always answer questions honestly.

Tell me about yourself? Explain:

- Where you go to school
- The kinds of classes you take
- Extracurricular activities
- Memberships: For example, National Honor Society, DECA, Junior Achievement, etc.
- Volunteer skills and experience and/or examples of how you help your neighbors, parents, or grandparents
- Jobs you do around the house
- Grades (if good)

Why do you want to work here?

- "I'm saving for college."
- "I'm earning money to buy a car."
- "I've heard that you are well respected in the community and I'd like a chance to work for you."

What is your greatest strength or weakness?
This answer should be tailored to the particular job.

- "I love working with people."
- "I'm a hard worker and willing to learn new things."
- "My greatest weakness is _____ but I'm willing to learn."

NOTES:

Tell me about your previous work experience.

Here's how to answer if you've never had a job: If you have never worked outside of your home and someone asks you about this in an interview, you can answer with:

- "I have never had an official job; however, my work ethic is strong, I get my homework done on time, and I get good grades in school. I'm never late for school and rarely miss class. I help my parents around the house with regular chores and also help my grandparents with (list the chores) _____. I also volunteer at_____ doing (or helping with)_____."
- "I have also interned at _____ doing_____."
- "I'm excited to be able to learn new things."

What personal skills do you have that will make you a good employee?

- "I'm very patient. I have strong people skills and I'm a hard worker."
- "I get along well with others. I'm good at following directions, and I enjoy helping customers."

Is there anything else that you'd like to share?

- "I'm a hard worker and have the qualifications you are looking for. I'm very interested in this job." (only say this if this is true)
- SMILE and say, "I appreciate you interviewing me and giving me a chance. If you do choose to hire me I will always work hard and do a great job for you and your customers. Thank you."

KEEP YOUR JOB

Skills taught at home, school, and in extracurricular activities or clubs are many of the same skills used in the work place. Have your teen list an example of how they would apply each of the following accomplishments in a work environment.

Follow Directions

EXAMPLE: I label my school papers as directed by my teacher.

_____

_____

Communicate Clearly

EXAMPLE: I use complete sentences when I communicate.

_____

_____

Be on Time

EXAMPLE: I am ready to leave for school on time.

_____

_____

Be Enthusiastic

EXAMPLE: I help with chores around the house without grumbling.

_____

_____

Practice Self-Control

EXAMPLE: I control my temper at chess club.

_____

_____

Take Responsibility for Assigned Tasks

EXAMPLE: I make sure to practice my instrument the entire time every week.

_____

_____

Be Able to Work Without Supervision

EXAMPLE: I'm a responsible babysitter to children of all ages.

_____

_____

Be Respectful

EXAMPLE: I'm kind and considerate to my fellow classmates, teammates, neighbors, and others. I don't participate in bullying.

_____

_____

Accept Instruction Eagerly

EXAMPLE: I ask questions when I don't understand an assignment or task at school.

_____

_____

Chapter 5

Overcome Stress

OVERCOME STRESS EVALUATION
From Chapter 2 of the book *Smile & Succeed for Teens*

Your teen will become familiar with methods to help them overcome stress.

- Have your teen fill out the **OVERCOME STRESS EVALUATION WORKSHEET** on the next page.

QUICK TIP: Focus on deep breathing. Take in as much air as you can—all the way down to your mid-section. Exhale and release the air slowly and evenly. It's relaxing. Feel that stress melt away.

☺ OVERCOME STRESS EVALUATION WORKSHEET

Your teen will discuss which stress management tools they use, how the tools help them, and give examples of when these tools are used. Example: I take a yoga class and it helps relieve my stress and also gives me a great workout.

Place a ✔ on the lines that apply to each tip presented in "Here's How" Chapter 2, pages 44-45 in *Smile & Succeed for Teens*. If possible, give specific examples of how you use each technique.

1. Think positively

____ I Use It ____ It Works ____ Will Try It

_____

2. Exercise

____ I Use It ____ It Works ____ Will Try It

_____

3. Read

____ I Use It ____ It Works ____ Will Try It

_____

4. New hobby

____ I Use It ____ It Works ____ Will Try It

_____

5. Volunteer

____ I Use It ____ It Works ____ Will Try It

_____

6. Meditate

____ I Use It ____ It Works ____ Will Try It

_____

7. Deep breathing

____ I Use It ____ It Works ____ Will Try It

_____

8. Positive people

____ I Use It ____ It Works ____ Will Try It

_____

9. Find humor

____ I Use It ____ It Works ____ Will Try It

_____

10. Forgive & forget

____ I Use It ____ It Works ____ Will Try It

_____

11. Friends/family time

____ I Use It ____ It Works ____ Will Try It

_____

12. Recognize change

____ I Use It ____ It Works ____ Will Try It

_____

13. Break up tasks

____ I Use It ____ It Works ____ Will Try It

_____

14. Ask for help

____ I Use It ____ It Works ____ Will Try It

_____

Don't let stress get the best of you!

Chapter 6

Master Electronic Etiquette

USE ELECTRONICS RESPONSIBLY
From Chapter 3 of the book *Smile & Succeed for Teens*

Your son or daughter will learn appropriate electronic etiquette for email, texting, and social media. They will then write their own professional emails, texts, and social media postings.

- Share examples of poorly written messages and have them identify and edit areas in need of work.

- Have them write an email, a text message, and a social media post for situations they have experienced using the example scenarios on the next three pages: needing make-up work, missing a practice, and communicating with customers via social media.

Be certain to go over

→ **TURN OFF THE** ←
ELECTRONICS

on pages 12-14 in the book
Smile & Succeed for Teens
with your teen to make certain
they understand the guidelines
for electronic etiquette.

SMART TIP: To create a cell phone contract for your teen visit www.smilethebook.com and click on "FREE."

QUICK TIP: As their parent, your son or daughter looks to you as a role model for how to act with electronics. Make sure you are following the advice in TURN OFF THE ELECTRONICS and MASTER ELECTRONIC ETIQUETTE in *Smile & Succeed for Teens*.

EMAIL SCENARIO

Jane Johnson was absent yesterday and needs to find out what she missed in her English class.

Inappropriate Email Message:

Subject Line: Hey!

Hey Smith!

Sorry I missed ur class yesterday, I was real sick from some food we ate last night. Not fun. I don't want this to mess with my grad though. I'm taking some medicine and hope 2 b back real soon. Just wanted to let u know what was up. Hope I didn't miss anything!

Thanx, J

Professionally Written Email Message:

Subject Line: Jane Johnson, English 1. Missed class today

Dear Mrs. Smith,

I am sorry that I was unable to attend English class today (Monday, December 8). I understand from a classmate that a study guide for Friday's exam was distributed. Would it be possible for me to pick up the study guide after school tomorrow between 3:00 p.m. and 4:00 p.m.? Could we please go over anything that I missed at that time? I do not want to fall behind in the class due to my absence. I appreciate your time and look forward to speaking with you soon.

Thank you,

Jane Johnson
English 1

TEXT MESSAGE SCENARIO

Alex Collins missed soccer practice today and needs to contact the coach.

Inappropriate Text Message:

I missd soccer 2day. Sry. C u to morow!

Professionally Written Text Message:

Dear Mr. Smith,

I am sorry I missed soccer practice today. I will be at soccer practice tomorrow at 3:00 p.m. sharp and will make sure I don't miss any more practices for the rest of the season. I realize that I will have to sit out during the first part of our game on Saturday since I missed one practice, according to our rules, and I understand that.

Thank you,

Alex Collins

SOCIAL MEDIA SCENARIO #1
Mia is asked to post something to attract customers on the social media site of the restaurant where she works part-time.

Inappropriate Social Media Post:
Spcl on Chkn Tndrs 2 day! Jst $399. WE R THE BEST. See ya!!!!!

Professionally Written Social Media Post:
Hungry? Chicken Tender special today: Just $3.99! Hope to see you soon. Thank you, valued customers!

SOCIAL MEDIA SCENARIO #2
Amy works part-time selling women's clothing, and is in charge of the business's social media accounts. A customer, Sharon, has posted the following question on their social media site: "I'm looking for the Brighton dress in black in a size 8. Do you have it in stock?"

Inappropriate Social Media Post:
Simply ignore the question and don't respond.

Inappropriate Social Media Post:
Yep, got it!

Professionally Written Social Media Post (responding the same day):
Hello, Sharon,

Yes, we have the size 8 Brighton dress in black in stock. Do you have any other questions? We look forward to seeing you.

Thank you, Amy

☺ SOCIAL MEDIA TIPS

Be nice. As explained in the Golden Rule in *Smile & Succeed for Teens*, treat people the way you'd like to be treated.

Never post or share anything mean or threatening.

Live your life. Don't let social media consume you. Put away your electronics for a while and get outside. Go for a walk. Read. Get a new hobby. Walk your dog. Volunteer.

Don't post when you are angry.

Watch your time. Set time limits for how long you want to stay online. Time seems to go by quickly when you are online. Don't waste the best years of your life on social media.

Stay safe. Don't chat with strangers, especially adults.

Never share personal information online. Stay safe. You never know who you are chatting with online.

Don't send pictures to people you don't know.

Spend more time in person with friends, family, and co-workers. Face-to-face communication will always be much more rewarding and make you feel better than any conversation you have online.

Learn more tips at www.smilethebook.com and click on "FREE."

QUICK TIP: Be proactive. As their parent, be certain to monitor your teen's Internet usage and access on all their electronics devices. Ensure privacy settings are updated. You may want to set time limits and have your teen turn in their electronics to you every evening.

Chapter 7

Deliver Amazing Customer Service

ROLE-PLAY CUSTOMER SERVICE SKILLS
From Chapter 4-6 of the book *Smile & Succeed for Teens*

Role-playing lets your teen experience first-hand how it feels when customer service is poor and when customer service is excellent.

After reading chapters 4-6 in *Smile & Succeed for Teens*, your teen will develop their people skills by participating in various customer service role-playing scenarios.

- Assign a customer service scenario to your teen using the **CUSTOMER SERVICE SCENARIOS** on the next page.

- Practice the scenario with your teen. Your teen should first role-play the "wrong way" to demonstrate how NOT to interact with customers. Then role-play the same scene using the methods in *Smile & Succeed for Teens* to delight customers. Correct and assist as needed. Immediately after each demonstration, take a few minutes to evaluate the role-play based on knowledge of the customer service and sales techniques in *Smile & Succeed for Teens*.

- Evaluate your teen's understanding of the techniques in *Smile & Succeed for Teens*.

QUICK TIP: Once your teen learns the skills in *Smile & Succeed for Teens*, encourage him or her to practice their new skills by volunteering. For example, many animal rescue groups hold adoption events on weekends at local businesses and often need volunteers. Animal shelters are another great place for teens to volunteer. Your teen can greet visitors and help them choose the right animal to adopt. A teen volunteer with good customer service skills can be a valuable asset to relieve busy staff and get more animals adopted!

CUSTOMER SERVICE SCENARIOS

NOTE: Chapters refer to chapters in the book *Smile & Succeed for Teens*

MAKE A COPY OF THIS PAGE AND CUT OUT THE SCENARIOS BELOW:
Put scenarios in a hat and have your teen pick each one out.

✂

....

A new customer enters your place of business. You are already helping someone else. **Ch. 4**

....

You spot a customer who seems to need help, and no one else is around. **Ch. 4**

....

You are volunteering at a local food bank called Helping Hands. The phone at the food bank is ringing and you answer it. (Answer with a SMILE!) **Ch. 4**

....

A person calls a nonprofit organization where you are volunteering. They would like to make a donation using a credit card, but you do not know if that is acceptable. **Ch. 4**

....

You are completing a transaction with a customer who has change coming back. **Ch. 4**

....

You are working at a sporting goods store. A customer comes in and says they are "just looking." **Ch. 5**

....

A customer comes into the produce market where you work. They are looking for the bulk food area. **Ch. 5**

....

You are working in a restaurant and a customer asks to make a change in one of the menu choices. You do not know if this is possible. **Ch. 5**

....

You are working at a retail store and helping a customer who is looking for a new television. You have answered their questions and guided them to the best television to meet their needs. They seem very interested and ready to buy. What do you do next? **Ch. 5**

....

A customer bought a shirt that did not match his suit. Process his return. **Ch. 6**

....

An unhappy customer returns to your bike shop with a tire that is still not holding air after being repaired. Handle the complaint. **Ch. 6**

....

ANSWER THE PHONE WITH A SMILE
From Chapter 4 of the book *Smile & Succeed for Teens*

Your teen will become familiar with phone etiquette and feel comfortable making calls to businesses and adults. They will also become comfortable answering the phone properly at a business.

- Model how you would talk on the phone (using a cell phone or your home phone) to a friend vs. a professional or customer.

- Have your teen practice with the sample dialogues on the next two pages. Have them use actual phones in different rooms so they can experience the call. Take turns with your teen being the employee and the customer.

- Have your son or daughter make a business phone call at home for a parent or other adult.

Good afternoon. Montgomery Inn. This is Alex. How may I help you?

Your smile "shines through" the phone line!

PIZZA ORDER SCENARIO

Employee: Good evening. Thank you for calling [pizza store name]. My name is Jane. Will this be pick up or delivery?

Customer: Hello, Jane. I'd like to order a pizza for pick up, please.

Employee: Okay, thank you. May I take your order, please?

Customer: Yes, I would like a [pizza choice] pizza with [toppings].

Employee: Will that be small, medium, or large?

Customer: [Small/Medium/Large], please.

Employee: Will that be all?

Customer: Yes, thank you.

Employee: You are welcome. Your total is $22.95. Your pizza will be ready in about 45 minutes. Thank you for ordering from [pizza store name].

Customer: You are welcome. Thank you.

Employee: You are welcome. Goodbye.

CLOSING TIME SCENARIO

Employee: Good evening. Thank you for calling [store name]. This is Tammy. How may I assist you today?

Customer: Hi, Tammy. What time are you open until tonight?

Employee: We are open tonight until 9:00 p.m.

Customer: Okay, thank you very much, Tammy.

Employee: You're welcome. Is there anything else that I can help you with?

Customer: No, that is all. Thank you again and have a great evening.

Employee: You are welcome, thank you. We hope to see you tonight.

Customer: Goodbye.

Employee: Goodbye.

ANSWER THE PHONE WITH A SMILE
SAMPLE DIALOGUES

CHECKING ON AN ITEM SCENARIO

Employee: Good afternoon. Thank you for calling [store name]. This is Tim. How may I assist you today?

Customer: Hi, Tim. How are you doing today?

Employee: I'm doing very well, thank you. How about yourself?

Customer: I am well, thanks. I was wondering if you have [item] in stock?

Employee: I do not know, off hand, if the item is in. Let me go check the sales floor and if necessary, the stock room. Could I please put you on hold for a couple of minutes so I can go check?

Customer: Absolutely. Thank you.

Employee: You are welcome, thank you. I'll be right back.

Employee: [after a couple of minutes] Hello, thank you for holding. I checked and we do have the item in stock.

Customer: Great. I'll come in sometime and look at it.

Employee: That sounds fine. Is there anything else I can help you with?

Customer: No, that is all. Thank you very much for your time.

Employee: You're welcome, thank you.

Customer: Goodbye.

Employee: Goodbye

CHECKING ON A MENU ITEM SCENARIO

Employee: Good morning. Becky's Cafe. This is ___(your name)___. How may I help you?

Customer: Do you have hot chocolate?

Employee: Yes, we do.

Customer: Thank you. I'll be over soon.

Employee: You're welcome. We look forward to seeing you. Thank you for calling.

Customer: You're welcome. 'Bye.

Employee: Thank you. Goodbye.

BE A MYSTERY SHOPPER ACTIVITY
From Chapters 1-7 of the book *Smile & Succeed for Teens*

Your teen will put their knowledge of the techniques in *Smile & Succeed for Teens* to use in a real-world setting. They will evaluate how sales associates and other employees conduct their business.

- Review the **BE A MYSTERY SHOPPER WORKSHEET** on the next page with them.

- Ask them to rate a business they frequent with your family using the **BE A MYSTERY SHOPPER WORKSHEET**.

- Have them compile their data and share the results with you.

- Ask them to identify which behaviors are exhibited more often and which ones are rarely seen.

- Have your teen summarize their Mystery Shopper experience.

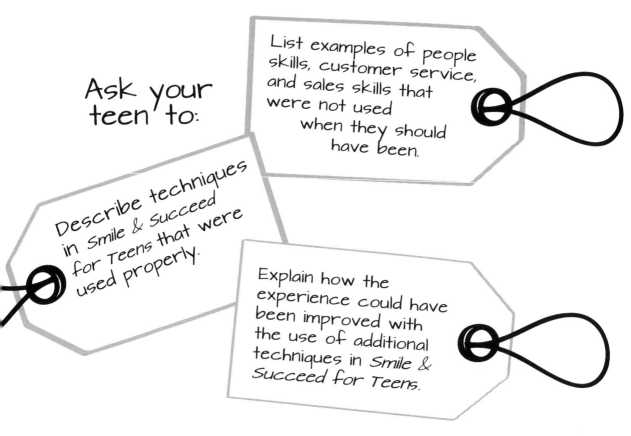

Ask your teen to:

List examples of people skills, customer service, and sales skills that were not used when they should have been.

Describe techniques in *Smile & Succeed for Teens* that were used properly.

Explain how the experience could have been improved with the use of additional techniques in *Smile & Succeed for Teens*.

☺ BE A MYSTERY SHOPPER WORKSHEET

Customer Service Techniques

Place an ✔ on the lines as you observe the correct use of a customer service or sales skill. Place an ✘ on the lines when an employee did not use a good customer service or sales skill, or poorly used a technique or skill. Discuss this information with your parent. You may want to take additional notes on employee actions that really impressed you or negative actions that might keep customers from returning to this business. The chapters refer to chapters in the book *Smile & Succeed for Teens*.

Name of Business: _____

Date: _____   **Time:** _____

Accompanied by: _____

Chapter One
____ Smile and say "Hello"
____ Make Good Eye Contact
____ Electronics Off
____ Say Please and Thank You
____ Shake Hands Firmly
____ Pay Attention (Listen)
____ Be Enthusiastic
____ Ask Questions
____ Proper Body Language

Chapter Three
____ Call People by Name
____ Be Prepared: The Six P's
____ Dress for Success
____ Keep it Professional
____ Master Electronic Etiquette
____ Learn Your Business
____ Make it Easy for Customers to do Business with You
____ Follow Up

Chapter Four
____ Acknowledge New Customers
____ Help Customers Promptly
____ Answer the Phone with a Smile
____ Hold, Please: Ask Permission First
____ Give Change Carefully

Chapter Five
____ "Just Looking:" Let Them Browse and Shop
____ Never Ask "Can I Help You?"
____ Don't Point - Walk and Show
____ When You Don't Know the Answer, Ask
____ Ask for the Sale - Then Stop Talking

Chapter Six
____ Handle Returns Graciously
____ Turn Complainers into Advocates

ADDITIONAL COMMENTS:

_____

_____

_____

Chapter 8

Volunteer Effectively

BOOST YOUR FUNDRAISING SKILLS
From Chapter 7 of the book *Smile & Succeed for Teens*

Volunteering at a Charity Event

In order to raise money, you have to ask for it. The following fundraising tips will help your teen improve his or her confidence and raise more money at charity events.

Role-play the following scenario with your teen using the tips in the bullet points below:

> Your teen is volunteering for a nonprofit at a local farmers' market. The farmers' market is busy so many prospective donors are walking by the table. The nonprofit's objective at this event is to raise visibility and funds. Take turns with your teen role-playing as the volunteer, and as the prospect.

- Smile, make eye contact, say hello, engage, and listen to your prospect. Be welcoming, knowledgeable, and confident.

- Stand up. People will feel much more at ease approaching you if you are standing and it's more professional.

- Keep your cell phone off and out of sight. Better yet, leave your cell phone at home.

- Never eat at your table.

- Don't chat with your co-volunteers when prospects are present, unless you are involving the prospect in your conversation.

- Listen to your prospect's needs and wants.

- Answer any questions.

- Tell a story. Share a short 30-second compelling success story with your prospects about the impact your nonprofit is making.

- Ask for the donation.

ROLE-PLAY: ASK FOR THE DONATION
From Chapter 7 of the book *Smile & Succeed for Teens*

Your teen will practice, get comfortable with, and test their fundraising skills.

- Help your teen brainstorm about their interests or passions, and locate a fundraising opportunity that is a match. Have them research this cause and the organization's programs.

- With this background knowledge, your teen will write brief dialogues following the fundraising models in ASK FOR THE DONATION-THEN STOP TALKING on pages 108-109 in *Smile & Succeed for Teens*.

- Have your teen role-play this dialogue with you or another teen. Correct and adjust as needed.

QUICK TIP: Your teen may be in a position to test their fundraising skills in the real world! For example, a charity may hold a local event where they need help fundraising. Encourage your teen to contact the organization to learn more and volunteer if possible.

MAKE AN IMPACT: VOLUNTEER
From Chapter 7 of the book *Smile & Succeed for Teens*

Teens are often unaware that their skills can help change the world. Let your teen know they can use their new skills to make a difference by volunteering for a cause that is important to them.

Ask your teen the following question:
"If you could volunteer for any nonprofit organization, which would it be? Think about types of causes you are interested in: people, animals, and/or the environment."

> ✦ Have your teen create a list of organizations he or she is interested in.

> ✦ Ask them to pick one organization from the list to explore using the steps below:

1. Is the organization a legitimate nonprofit?

2. Does the organization have effective programs in place?

3. Search the name of the nonprofit organization online for recent news coverage to learn more about them and to uncover any questionable activities.

4. What are the volunteer opportunities with this organization?

5. Does the organization offer a variety of ways to volunteer?

6. Can your teen help the organization raise funds?

7. Have your teen contact the organization to discuss ways he or she can help.

8. Have your teen report back to you and choose a way to volunteer and raise funds.

Your teen can get started volunteering and fundraising for this nonprofit.

QUICK TIP: Look for flexible volunteer opportunities that are one-time opportunities, like a one or two-hour time commitment at a special event or a task your teen can complete from home. This way your teen can evaluate the opportunity before making a long term commitment.

Chapter 9

Make it Stick

WHAT HAVE YOU LEARNED?
From Chapters 1-7 of the book *Smile & Succeed for Teens*

Here's a fun way to review *Smile and Succeed for Teens* with your teen when you don't have a lot of time. Inspirational quotes and illustrations with captions are found throughout the book and support the content.

- Ask your teen to choose their favorite three quotes from the book and discuss why they like them. Have them explain the connection to the content in *Smile & Succeed for Teens* and why the quote is important.

- Ask your teen to choose their favorite facts from the book. The facts appear on the illustrations of the computer screen. Have your teen discuss these facts with you and why they are important.

The most common mistake new employees make is not dressing professionally.

- Point to each illustration in the book and read the caption. Then ask them: "What does this mean to you?"

Add meaning to your life - create good friendships.

QUICK TIP: Take a few minutes to review *Smile & Succeed for Teens* with your teen each day or every week. Choose one or two concepts to highlight and practice each time to keep them at their best.

☺ FUN QUIZ: TEST YOUR TEEN'S KNOWLEDGE

From Chapters 1-7 of the book *Smile & Succeed for Teens*

The following questions will test your teen's knowledge. Give your teen the fun quiz below (page numbers refer to the page where the answer can be found in *Smile and Succeed for Teens*):

- How long does it take to create a first impression? **p. 8**

- Name three of The Top Ten People Skills. **p. 8-27**

- How do the most positive conversations happen? **p. 11**

- What can you focus on if you feel uncomfortable looking someone in the eye? **p. 10**

- How long do text messages and online posts last? **p. 13**

- Students with high scoring handshakes are identified as_____. **p. 18**

- What is the golden rule? **p. 19**

- Describe proper body language. **p. 27**

- How can good references help you get a job? **p. 34**

- Name five ways to prepare for an interview. **p. 37-38**

- List five ways to overcome stress. **p. 43-45**

- What percentage of teens report having difficulty sleeping due to stress? **p. 44**

- What are the "Six P's?" **p. 52**

- Describe how to dress for success. **p. 54-55**

- Why is electronic etiquette important? **p. 58-59**

- How quickly should you answer a customer's email? **p. 64**

- What percent of small business customers will make their purchases at another shop if they feel the sales staff doesn't care? **p. 69**

- What percentage of how you're perceived on the phone is based solely on the tone of your voice? **p. 72**

- Name one reason why you should volunteer. **p. 103-104**

- How can you overcome the fear of fundraising? **p. 105-106**

FINAL WRAP UP!:

Write down one valuable social or job skill you learned from role-playing the scenarios.

_____

_____

_____

What's the most important thing to do when a customer enters your business?

    A.   Ignore them

    B.   Smile and say hello

    C.   Get out your cell phone and start texting

    D.   Talk with co-workers

CORRECT ANSWER: B. Smile and say hello

QUICK TIP: Use these questions whenever you want to test your teen. Use them in the car, after school, or anytime you can fit them in.

REVIEW THE BOOK *SMILE & SUCCEED FOR TEENS*
From Chapters 1-7 of the book *Smile & Succeed for Teens*

Now it's time for your teen to review the book. *Say to your teen*: "Today you are going to put your book reviewer hat on and review your copy of *Smile & Succeed for Teens*."

This exercise is designed to get your teen to talk about the book by providing an overview of what they've learned. One of the best ways to assess how much content your teen has retained is by asking them to review it. Have your teen write or discuss with you a review of the book including such things as:

✦ A short summary

✦ The three most useful parts

✦ What they learned from the book

✦ What they will use from the book

✦ Advice for other readers

Next, have your teen take a piece of paper and number it 1-5. Ask them to write five additional tips they learned from the book.

Finally, have your teen write a review of *Smile & Succeed for Teens* for submitting to the newspaper, the school paper, and to use as a writing sample.

BOOK REPORT

Ask your teen to write a two-minute book report about *Smile & Succeed for Teens* and share it with you and his or her teacher and classmates. Book reports don't have to be boring. They can be fun and creative!

There are many formats for writing a book report:

- Standard book report
- Standard book report plus PowerPoint
- Short video
- Radio ad
- Poem
- Comic strip
- Collage
- Picture

Book reports are an effective way for your teen to practice the communication skills he or she learned in *Smile & Succeed for Teens*. Remind your teen to be prepared for questions and to have fun.

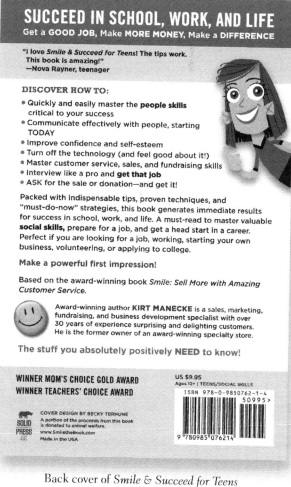

Back cover of *Smile & Succeed for Teens*

FREE COMMUNICATION, CUSTOMER SERVICE, SALES, AND FUNDRAISING TIPS FROM KIRT MANECKE

I hope you find this Parent's Guide valuable to help you get even more out of your investment in *Smile & Succeed for Teens*. To access lots of valuable free tips and resources to help teens succeed, be sure to visit www.smilethebook.com and click on "FREE." Also be sure to visit my blog at www.smilethebook.com/blog/ or visit www.smilethebook.com and click on "BLOG".

www.smilethebook.com

ABOUT THE AUTHOR

 **KIRT MANECKE** is an award-winning author and a sales, marketing, fund-raising, and business development specialist with over 30 years of experience making customers smile. A proven "natural" salesman, Kirt helps companies build lasting, profitable relationships with clients through strategic marketing and expert customer service.

As founder and former owner of an award-winning specialty retail business in Michigan, Kirt created and implemented an innovative six-week training program that maximized customer satisfaction and sales by teaching employees many of the skills presented in his award-winning first book, *Smile: Sell More with Amazing Customer Service*. Many of these skills have been customized for teens and included in *Smile & Succeed for Teens*.

In his free time, Kirt volunteers his skills to help end animal cruelty and preserve natural spaces in the United States and abroad. Kirt is founder and chair of the Michigan chapter of Animals Asia, a group devoted to rescuing animals from cruelty, raising awareness, and improving public policy affecting animals. Kirt lives in Milford, Michigan.

Learn more about Kirt at www.SmiletheBook.com.

NOTES

NOTES

NOTES

NOTES

NOTES

NOTES

31293765R00040

Made in the USA
San Bernardino, CA
03 April 2019